THE ... RIES

CW01627837

Violence in the Workplace

What is it? How should it be dealt with?
What is a Christian response?

Michael Fitzsimons

kevin mayhew

kevin mayhew

First published in Great Britain in 2009 by Kevin Mayhew Ltd
Buxhall, Stowmarket, Suffolk IP14 3BW
Tel: +44 (0) 1449 737978 Fax: +44 (0) 1449 737834
E-mail: info@kevinmayhewltd.com

www.kevinmayhew.com

9 8 7 6 5 4 3 2 1 0

ISBN 978 1 84867 120 1
Catalogue No. 1501158

Cover design by Rob Mortonson
Edited by Delian Bower and Katherine Laidler
Typeset by Richard Weaver and Chris Coe

Printed and bound in Great Britain

Contents

About the author

Michael Fitzsimons is a Catholic priest. He is currently assistant priest at the parish of Christ the King and Our Lady in Liverpool. Prior to entering the priesthood Michael trained as a youth and community worker and has experience of working with young people and adults in a wide variety of settings, including projects working with homeless people, detached youth work, community projects and prisons.

Introduction

Jocelyn Bryan and Brendan Geary

If you have picked up or bought this booklet then the chances are that you have a concern about a difficult situation in your family, workplace, church, organisation – or in your own life – and are not sure what to do about it. On the other hand, you may be in a teaching or leadership position and want to find a resource to help you with your job. Whatever has aroused your interest, it suggests that you are aware of a particular area of concern and would like to be better informed. If you come from a Christian background, you may also wonder about doing the 'right' thing in terms of your values and beliefs. This booklet, and the others in the series, have been written with you in mind.

All of us can be faced with a range of problems that do not admit to easy solutions. The complexity of our lives and the range of problems that we encounter make the task of management especially difficult. Large organisations can call on the qualified and experienced members of personnel and legal departments to assist in these situations. People in smaller organisations – small businesses, family firms, churches, schools, voluntary organisations and community projects, for example – often do not have these resources available to help deal with and navigate their way through the difficulties and competing needs and responsibilities of those involved.

This booklet is one of a series which was originally published in *The Christian handbook of abuse, addiction and difficult behaviour.* The following topics were selected as they are ones which many of us now find ourselves having to deal with, or which are regularly presented to us by the media:

- Child sexual abuse
- Partner violence
- Addiction to drugs and alcohol
- Gambling addiction
- Sexual addiction and internet pornography
- Difficult people
- Adult bullying
- Violence in the workplace.

Issues like alcohol abuse or the problems of working with 'difficult people', have been part of human experience for a long time. Some of them, however, like child abuse, adult bullying or partner violence, were not spoken about, and society, families, churches and organisations colluded in denying that they existed. The problems of internet pornography are a new manifestation of an old problem, but the ease of access of the internet has led to this, and gambling addiction, becoming an issue that can potentially touch almost every household in the country. Violence has always been a risk in some occupations, but in recent years it has become a present concern and danger for people who previously did not have to worry much about personal safety.

The first stage in dealing with anything is to try to understand the problem. Accordingly, each of these booklets begins with a discussion of the topic being addressed. For example, in the booklet on child sexual abuse, there is a discussion on the prevalence of child sexual abuse, the effects on victims, the different kinds of abuse and the characteristics of perpetrators. The topics covered in these booklets often lead to an instinctive withdrawal, or possibly revulsion. In attempting to understand the problem it is hoped that we begin to see the person who is the source of our problem not so much as a difficult (violent or abusive) person, but more as a person with difficulties. This has the advantage of releasing compassion and empathy, and encouraging us to engage strategies to help the person rather than simply label them as problematic.

The second stage is to ask what we can do about it. Each booklet has a section on how to respond, with the best available information about possible therapeutic approaches. There are also lists of 'do's' and 'don'ts' at the end of each booklet which may provide some practical advice on how to deal with the issue. At the end of the booklet you will find a reflection on what a Christian response might be to this particular problem. These are not exhaustive discussions, but are there to offer pointers which may help to illuminate and offer insight to the questions which can arise in a rather dark place. Those who are interested in a more developed discussion may benefit from reading Alan Bartlett's chapter on Practical Theology in *The Christian handbook of abuse, addiction and difficult behaviour.*

Each booklet contains a short section on care of self. This section has been written with leaders in mind. We realise that these booklets may be read by people who are not in leadership positions. It should not be difficult to make the necessary adjustments in order to apply the wise and practical advice offered in this section to your own situation. It has been included in each booklet as those who find themselves dealing with difficult and challenging situations can become stretched in terms of time, energy, relationships and personal resources. In order to help other people, you need to be in a healthy condition yourself. All of us have resources that enable us to rise to meet the challenges of a difficult situation, but, at the same time, very few of us can continue to manage without the support of others, and sensible choices that enable us to care for our selves.

We hope that you find this booklet informative, practical, insightful and helpful. If it provides an incentive to seek help, or information that enables you to understand better a difficult situation, or some thoughtful reflection on the issues involved, then we will have fulfilled our task.

Violence in the Workplace

Michael Fitzsimons

Recently, when disposing of the junk 'mail' which regularly clogs up our office fax machine, one of the papers caught my attention: in-between debt collection and hire car offers there was a crime management firm advertising security services. This is not unusual until you consider its headline, which targeted organisations seemingly at risk from anti-social behaviour. It listed schools and educational establishments, public transport, empty properties, parks and then, perhaps surprisingly, churches. Having worked in the voluntary sector for a number of years, I was accustomed to thinking about these issues but initially I was surprised that now churches would be seen as prime targets for such services. Then almost immediately I began to reflect on how the current church premises I work from have regularly been subjected to vandalism. Groups of young people often gather in or nearby the churches and church houses in the area where I live and cause disturbances. Indeed there has been a growth of violence and violent attacks made on clergy and other church workers in recent years. It was not hard to bring to mind numbers of situations known to me personally where clergy had suffered from intimidation, theft, burglary and, occasionally, violent attacks. Perhaps I shouldn't have been surprised by this fax at all.

The issue of violence and aggression is current in our society and generates much discussion as to its causes and its perceived growth. Acts of violence and aggression directed against caring professionals, including clergy and other pastoral workers, are seemingly more commonplace and often attract significant media attention and wide coverage. This both serves to highlight the issue but also potentially increases fear of such attacks which generally, thankfully, are still not commonplace. However, it should encourage us to think critically about the threat of aggression and violence in our workplaces and pastoral activities, and actively consider steps to promote safety and well-being of employees, clergy, pastoral workers and those who work in the voluntary sector. What can be done to further understand this problem and how can we make an effective response?

What is violence in the workplace?

We often make various assumptions about violence and aggression in terms of both what it actually is and also what causes a person to become violent and aggressive. Some of these assumptions can be helpful but often they do not take the full situation into account. Firstly let us consider defining violence. We may assume that an act of violence is when someone is physically harmed, but what about intimidation or threat, which can be equally debilitating and cause equal fear? We may assume that all violence is intentional, but must we then consider whether sometimes the aggressor is out of control due to the influence of alcohol or drugs or simply at the end of their tether? Maybe we would want to say that all violence is unjust or unfair but how do we define legitimate self-defence?

In reality, violence is a more widespread phenomenon than we might at first imagine. Let us think of the many times when we are asked to offer pastoral care to individuals or groups we would consider to be 'victims' of violence. This may include situations of abuse, domestic violence, neighbour threats and intimidation, violent crime, racial or homophobic harassment, working with asylum seekers or refugees fleeing institutional or political violence to name just a few. Any definition would need to include direct physical violence and threat of violence but also the wider social, structural and cultural aspects of violence. Engage[1] offers one possible definition:

> Violence is any physical, emotional, verbal, institutional, structural or spiritual behaviour, attitude, policy or condition that diminishes, dominates or destroys ourselves or others.[2]

This definition then continues by recognising that violence is motivated by fear, anger, greed or the desire to control and dominate, but also at times can be motivated by frustration in the face of perceived injustice, or used by people with the conviction that they are attempting to overcome past violence directed towards them, and that there is no other way. It also

1. Engage is a study programme and a project of *Pace e Bene* Nonviolence Service, Las Vegas, Nevada, USA.
2. Definition from *Engage* in Slattery, L., Butigan, K., Pelicaric, V., and Preston-Pile, K. (2005). *Engage: Exploring Nonviolent Living; A study program for learning, practicing and experimenting with the power of creative nonviolence to transform our lives and our world* (Oakland, California: Pace e Bene Press).

notes that violence often provokes new and additional violence in a spiral of retaliation.

The reasons why individuals resort, deliberately or otherwise, to aggression, violence, intimidation and threat are myriad and potentially complex. It is possible to identify and summarise up to eight possible groupings of theories about the causes of aggression and violence.[1]

1. Natural or innate theories see aggression as a natural part of every animal and indeed every human being. Humans, as the most dominant species, are the most aggressive of all and are the only group who will fight over an idea or a belief, and furthermore we are continuing this need to dominate by destroying ourselves in warfare. More positively viewed, these theories propose that aggression can be used to survive difficult situations and challenges in life.

2. The frustration theory proposes that people become aggressive when their needs are not met and this is a response to the frustration generated. The frustration is relieved, permanently or at least temporarily, once the aggressive act is over.

3. Behavioural theories suggest that aggression is a learned process. Behaviour is controlled by past experiences and the consequences derived from those experiences. If someone has learnt that the use of aggression and violence achieves their aims and desires, there is no incentive to change.

4. Ecological theories note that people are affected by the conditions in which they live. Some theories identify that people resort to violence when food, air or space is scarce. Environmental factors such as overcrowding, poor lighting, shabby furniture, enforced use of shared or inadequate facilities can all contribute to aggressive behaviour.

5. Sociological theories identify the causes of aggression and violence as being rooted in culture, roles and stereotypes created

1. Braithwaite, R. (2001). *Managing Aggression* (London/New York: Routledge/CommunityCare).

by and within society. The potential for conflict and aggression is increased when socicty distributes its resources based on stereotypical norms (class, gender, ethnicity, educational achievement, accent) and thus they are distributed unequally.

6. Psychodynamic theories place emphasis on the influence of our past and how others, particularly significant relationships, related to us. Being constantly told as children that we were bad or naughty, or regularly and unfavourably compared with siblings or others, can have a significant impact on our lives. Not having the skills to give this appropriate expression as children or when tired or frustrated, aggressive behaviour is perceived as rebelliousness. The resultant reaction of parents or teacher reinforces the child's sense of 'badness'. Hence anger is bottled up, sometimes over many years, until it explodes in violent temper outbursts or can be triggered by someone, often an authority figure, who reminds us of our childhood protagonist.
7. Interactive theory understands violence as a process influenced by others. If we are hostile to another person, this may lead to hostility and aggression in them. Violent acts may then be perpetrated thus giving our initial aggression validity. This theory sees violence and aggression as a continual vicious circle of hostile acts and responses which deepen the initial hostility and aggression.
8. Finally, chemically induced theories propose that chemicals, be they introduced by use of alcohol or drugs, or certain foods that contain toxins, or produced internally due to physical illness or hormonal imbalance, can give rise to aggressive behaviour.

Added to this are certain behaviour patterns or actions which combine different and various aspects of some or all the theories identified above. However it is understood, most forms of violence and aggression do require a cause of some sort. We can stop and consider ourselves for a moment and think about what can make us angry, upset or nervous, and then ask ourselves what happens when this intensifies or escalates to a certain degree or level. Once we reach a particular threshold, most of us can feel aggressive or even potentially violent. If we are being honest, most of us can think of situations where we would at least be tempted to become aggressive, especially if we felt the aggression was justifiable in the context.

It is also possible to learn that if we use violence, we can get our own way. This can be from a very early age and we can observe the schoolyard bully learning that if you threaten someone with violence, then they may give you their sweets; if as an adult you walk into an advice project, community centre or church and patiently sit and wait your turn, someone will come to you, but if you walk in and start to shout and bang the tables with your fists, you are guaranteed the attention of at least one member of staff. Sadly some people have learnt that resorting to violence can get you what you want.

Violence against professionals

Violence against professionals in the community was the focus of research funded by the Economic and Social Research Council in 2001.[1] This study examined the nature and extent of violence and whether it was socially patterned by the professional's age or gender, and secondly how these professionals responded and managed both the threats and actual incidence of violence. The research focused on GPs, probation officers and Anglican clergy. The most common form of aggression reported was verbal abuse. 71% of clergy indicated that they had been verbally abused at least once over the previous two-year period. In the same period 22% of the Anglican clergy indicated that they had been threatened with violence, with those working in inner-city areas reporting a significantly higher incidence compared to those working in rural areas. Female clergy reported slightly fewer threats than males.

Across all the professional groups 10–12% reported being assaulted, with slightly higher levels of reporting amongst the clergy. For the most part these assaults involved being pushed or shoved without injury. Some

1. www.esrcsocietytoday.ac.uk

key differences emerged for the clergy who reported these assaults. While the majority of assaults on GPs and probation officers occurred in their main place of work, most assaults on clergy were in their homes, on the street or local estates rather than in or near church buildings. Whereas the majority of GPs knew their assailant, almost half the clergy reported being assaulted by someone not known to them. All the professional groups reported that being assaulted affected the way they dealt with clients and made them feel less secure. Given that many of the clergy had experienced assault in their home, there is potential for these feelings of insecurity to be higher.

It is interesting to consider what the research tells us regarding the varied responses from different professional groups to such violence and aggression. The fluidity and elusive nature of some risks, combined with the complex working relationships between professionals and the people they work with and how they understand such relationships, was significant. The clergy, alongside GPs, were the least likely to use formal risk assessment procedures, utilising these measures much more haphazardly and reactively. The increase of women clergy in the past few years may also be a significant factor. Although this research focused on Anglican clergy, there is a growing presence of women working in pastoral care in all the Churches. In fact, the majority of workers in lay-led initiatives tend to be women. The presence of women has challenged conventional working practices such as making late-night home visits alone which perhaps assumed the presence of male clergy. Women in all three professions reported both higher fears of violence and being more likely to take precautions on a regular basis. The reported incidence of threats and assaults was lower for women than for their male colleagues.

A number of commentators within different Churches responded to this research by associating aggression and violence with the alleged decline in respect for clergy, and indeed all professional groups in society. Interestingly, in the ESRC research there was a generational shift in this area, with older clergy and GPs explaining the rise in aggression due to a perceived loss of status. Younger clergy and GPs, on the other hand, were more likely to identify aggression in contextual terms such as the socio-economic or personal circumstances of the communities and individuals they serve, and possibly stressing a more egalitarian relationship between clergy and people.

This research corresponds with other evidence on violence in the workplace and specific research on threats against clergy. In 2006 Nick Tolson of National Churchwatch found that 48% of a sample of 90 clergy had suffered at least one violent assault in the preceding twelve months,[1] and other evidence suggests that certain occupations are at special risk, including nurses, social workers, those providing care and advice, and those who work alone.[2] You are more likely to face direct violence and aggression in the 'care' sector than in retail, banking or even the security sector.

Being aware of the complex nature of violence and aggression and the possible causes of such behaviour enables us to identify the elements over which we have some control. We can then start to formulate effective approaches both to reduce and minimise the risk of having to face such aggression and even strategies to confront and resist violence when it occurs.

1. Nick Tolson, 'The Clergy Lifestyle Theory,' at www.nationalchurchwatch.com
2. Chappell, D. and Di Martino, V. (2000). *Violence at Work* (2nd edition) (Geneva: International Labour Office).

How should it be dealt with?

Preventing or minimising the risk

The first response when considering the risk of encountering violence and aggression in our ministry and work is to reflect on how this risk can be prevented or minimised. There are two aspects to prevention: firstly examining the physical security of our buildings and homes (particularly as many clergy use their home as a place of work where they see various people in need); and secondly looking at safer working practices that will reduce the risk of violence or assault. Physical security measures can include considering:

- Security lighting
- Door entry systems
- Perimeter fencing
- CCTV
- Alarms and panic buttons

The use of door entry systems, CCTV, or a simple spyhole in a door can be both effective and relatively inexpensive. Where possible, also consider the layout and use of premises. Keep rooms near to the entrance for interviews, counselling and support, and, where possible, have more than one entry or door to these rooms. Think about the layout and use of furniture in the room – ensure that you can be seated nearest the door.

This also applies to counsellors, nurses or care workers who interview vulnerable adults, some of whom may be violent or under the influence of alcohol or drugs, or be suffering from a personality or organic disorder such as schizophrenia. Furnishings should be warm and welcoming but eradicate any unnecessary risks by the removal of heavy ashtrays or other ornaments that could be thrown or used as a weapon.

Having examined the physical safety of your premises, consider next your work practices and procedures. Are there ways of reducing risk? Firstly consider that you are much more at risk when you are working alone. This cannot always be avoided when offering one-to-one support or confidential services, but having someone else around in the house, church, office or project will significantly reduce your risk. The person does not have to be working directly with you but a colleague, receptionist, secretary, sacristan or church volunteer who may be doing other work will both reduce the risk and ensure that there is someone to raise the alarm if necessary. There is strong evidence that simply having another person present can significantly reduce the possibility of violent or aggressive behaviour, even if they are not trained, experienced or even expected to deal with any violent situation or threat.[1]

Often people in need call unexpectedly or 'out of hours,' but do consider whether this should be encouraged and whether it can be avoided. Think carefully about what you are actually able to do. Some organisations which offer 24-hour telephone support, for example, have a policy of not opening the door after a certain time at night. In cases of emergency, the police can be called. If you do allow someone entrance, consider telephoning a colleague or a parishioner, for example, and tell them that you are allowing someone in and ask them to call you back in 30 minutes. Similar arrangements can be put in place where clergy or care workers are 'on call' and asked to attend or visit other people's homes. A few practicalities should be borne in mind. Firstly always carry a mobile telephone and personal attack alarm, even if you know the people you are visiting. Remember, even if you know the person you are visiting, you do not know who else might be present – another family member, for example, or an ex-partner. Again, consider letting someone else know that you are going out to see someone, and tell them to phone you on your mobile phone at an agreed time, or inform them that you will contact them when you return.

These practices may initially seem excessive or overcautious, but they are basic common sense and would be expected of many other professionals working in community settings. Just consider the following scenario. One evening you have allowed someone in to your home who has arrived unexpectedly in a distressed state. You call a parishioner and ask them to call you in 15 minutes. When you return to attend to the visitor, he

1. Nick Tolson, 'The Clergy Lifestyle Theory' at www.nationalchurchwatch.com

has become more agitated and at times aggressive, and you feel uncomfortable and under threat. When the parishioner calls in 15 minutes, it allows you to leave the room to answer the phone. You can then decide if you need to call in extra help, or even contact the police if appropriate.

All this consideration of risk reduction and prevention of violent attack may seem contrary to the purpose of an organisation or the mission and ministry of clergy. Surely we want our places of employment, churches, church houses and projects to be places of welcome, highly accessible and open to all people and especially anyone in need of care or support? Focusing specifically on churches, we could be the safest church, presbytery, or rectory, with the safest work practices and procedures, but end up being distant, removed, inaccessible and entirely irrelevant to the communities we seek to serve and minister to. Equally, though, we also have a duty of care to ourselves and others who work and serve alongside us. We need to be aware of our limitations and feel able to say 'no' at times when we feel vulnerable or unsafe. Safety and risk reduction and accessibility and welcome are not diametrically opposed, but rather need to be in constant dialogue.

A word of warning, though: we can become over-reliant on technology without thinking what it will actually achieve. I remember reflecting once with staff in a local prison after an alarm bell had been triggered, which immediately resulted in radio contact with staff and a number of officers being present at the scene within seconds and minutes, with other specially trained and equipped staff potentially available quickly. I couldn't help but compare this with the homeless drop-in centre where I was then working. The centre also had an alarm bell which set off a loud and usefully distracting siren, but ultimately it still left me and four or five volunteers to deal with any potential incident of violence or aggression. Consideration can be given to the possibility of panic alarms and indeed personal alarms being automatically connected to police or security centres. This will be helpful in some settings, but simple over-reliance on technology, practical security measures and risk assessment is not enough.

Given that you have considered physical security and balanced that with the desire to be accessible and available, there is still the potential of having to deal with an unknown person, or indeed the known aggressive person who has turned up unexpectedly, until help can be summoned. In this section I will attempt to offer some practical, non-violent and realistic responses. I will try to offer ways of directly responding to an incident of violence and aggression directed at an individual.

Defusing the situation

The first task is to attempt to defuse the situation gently, slow things down and hopefully avoid actual violence. In reality, many violent or aggressive incidents occur very rapidly, giving you little time to think through a strategy or response. Here, therefore, I will examine any given violent or potentially violent encounter in 'slow motion', considering the assessment of the situation and those involved, responding, dealing and then managing the incident, and finally attempting to avoid escalating the situation and so bring it to a successful outcome.

When confronted with aggression, threat or actual violence, certain 'automatic' responses can immediately kick in. These can be typified by the fight, flight or freeze responses, which are all natural, biological, physiological responses to situations of fear, violence and aggression. Natural angers, fears, frustrations and panic quickly come to the surface when we are faced with such situations. Before we know it we are thinking and responding: 'How dare he speak to me like that, I'm going to give him a piece of my mind' or 'She has a knife – get out of here' or 'They're coming at me – what should I do?' Each of these responses is natural and understandable, and indeed is controlled by the automatic physiological changes that happen in situations of stress. (These same physiological factors are occurring in the aggressor, and these control and promote their behaviour and reactions.) While these initial responses are all understandable, they may not always be the most appropriate ways of responding to situations of conflict, aggression and violence.

Keeping calm

Initially it is essential to stay calm and to try and relax. This is easier said than done when faced with aggression, but it is achievable and essential to buy you time to make an effective assessment of your situation. The following steps will allow you to attempt to calm yourself and, as much as possible, to relax and stay in control of your mind and your body.

- Say STOP to yourself
- Breath in deeply, breath out slowly
- Drop your shoulders
- Relax your hands
- Do it again!

As has already been stated, we often spring into action when faced with violence. Just stopping ourselves from immediate reaction is the first step. Allowing ourselves to breath deeply and slowly is a powerful relaxation agent. This allows time to make an assessment of both the environment and the aggressor. First consider if there is any avenue of escape. No one should feel under any obligation to remain in a situation of violence or potential violence if they can legitimately remove themselves from it. If you can leave a room, do so, thereby preventing a person's access to you and potentially causing you harm. Remember that no threat to property or resources can be compared to any individual's personal safety and security. A second assessment is needed about whether anyone else is present.

- Who are they and how near are they?
- Are they people you have a responsibility for – service users, parishioners or colleagues? If you left, would they be in danger?
- Are they people who can help or summon assistance from, for example, the police?
- Are they also potential threats?

The presence of another person, whoever they might be, is a significant factor in reducing the threat of violence or assault.

The final factor to consider in your physical environment is whether there are any large objects such as desks or church benches that could serve as barriers. If someone is being verbally threatening from the other end of a large desk or table, I certainly will feel slightly better than if I am in a small room with only chairs, which is isolated from other rooms in the premises and where there is no effective barrier between myself and the aggressor.

The next assessment needed is of the threatening person themselves:

- Who is this person?
- Do you know them?
- What is your relationship?
- How near are they to you?
- What is their emotional state?
- What is being said and how?
- Is there evidence of alcohol or substance use?
- Do they possess any weapons such as a gun or a knife?

All this information is important for you as you try and remain calm and keep control of the situation. Any of the above information will help you make better-informed responses. It is more likely that you will know the aggressive person, as most reported incidents of violence are from people known to the victims. Evidence of alcohol or substance use can indicate that the person is more likely to resort to violence or aggression. But equally if they are highly intoxicated, it may be easier to make an escape if needed. As well as the possession of actual weapons, also consider the availability of any makeshift weapons such as smashed bottles, cutlery or lightweight furniture which could be thrown. Be aware that even objects we do not ordinarily consider as potential weapons, such as candlesticks or lamps, could very easily be used against us.

Communicating with the aggressor

Having made the fullest assessment possible, we now have to try and open communication with the aggressor. The most influential channel of communication will be non-verbal:

- Often it is all we have initially, but it is first and immediate.
- It buys time and can have a powerful calming effect.
- It accounts for approximately 75% of all we communicate!

There is a problem here as fear and violence look similar! Naturally you will feel fear or indeed aggression – you are in fight-or-flight mode, which is how we are 'hard-wired' to deal with threats to our person. Indeed most people would consider it reasonable to be fearful if someone is acting aggressively, especially if they are threatening actual physical harm. Naturally our bodies will want to communicate this fear or even our own aggression and defensiveness. The problem is that we ought not to show this fear but rather signal non-aggression. In other words we must teach our bodies to lie! Yes, we may feel fear but what we will try to display and signal is an attitude and position of non-aggression. Signalling non-aggression is powerful and also puts you in a position of strength, not weakness, while still resisting and confronting the violence. To signal non-violence:

- Create space
- Relax your posture
- Drop and extend your arms
- Open your hands
- Lower your voice
- Slow your movements

Having signalled non-aggression, we can now attempt to calm the situation. In all the following strategies it is worthwhile to note that we cannot solely calm and resolve this aggression and potential violence. This will take two parties – you and the aggressor. Remember all that has been said about non-verbal communication, which is still a primary tactic at this stage. We can, however, now start to encourage talking and use verbal communication ourselves. Offer reassurance where appropriate. While there remains a high potential for violence, at this stage no one has been physically hurt and the situation is not out of control. It has not gone too far and can still be resolved amicably. So often in my experience it has been possible to reassure an aggressor that things can still be managed and at this stage no sanction will need to be imposed. This was particularly the case while working in homeless projects and hostels when people often felt that they had nothing left to lose and they were sure they would be barred or evicted from the project. People engage in high-risk strategies when there is little to lose and a high-risk gamble appears to be worth taking. If people perceive that a change of attitude or behaviour may result in a better outcome, there is a higher likelihood of reducing the emotional temperature.[1] Hearing that, at this stage, it may be possible for them to remain and explain their need, often led to a defusing of tension and a reduction in the threat of violence.

It is essential when dealing with any incident of violence or aggression not to rush to resolve it or run ahead before the aggressor is starting to calm and engage with you. It is better to proceed gradually and surely. I can think of numerous situations when dealing with an incident of violence when I have made assumptions about how someone will respond without allowing them time to calm. This inevitably led to inflaming the situation further. A violent incident can often attract attention from many others present, which is not always helpful – consider a fight in a school yard which will soon attract a good crowd of children to observe, and even encourage, the fight. As a person starts to calm, consideration can be given to moving to a less public space to avoid an audience. Clearly we should never isolate ourselves with an aggressor but perhaps we can ask others present to back off a little or to continue with their normal activities. Finally, at all times continue to anticipate violence and ensure continuing vigilance. People who are aggressive rarely calm down in seconds or minutes and must be given appropriate time to relax and allow their aggression to dissipate.

Once a situation has been calmed, we can move to further stages of relating to the aggressive person and ultimately managing the situation.

1. Leith, K. P. and Baumeister, R. F. (1996). 'Why do bad moods increase self-defeating behavior? Emotion, risk-taking and self-regulation', *Journal of Personality and Social Psychology*, 71, 1250–1267.

We might not particularly feel like relating with someone who has threatened us, let alone dealing with them with understanding and warmth, but if we set it in the context of resolving the situation and protecting ourselves from further violence, it is a worthwhile thing to do. Try to encourage agreement and verbalise this with 'yes' statements that both of you can agree. Remember it takes both you *and* the aggressor to resolve the issue successfully without the use of violence and so use 'we' statements to agree that you can resolve the issue peacefully and that you don't wish to hurt or harm the other person. It is only at this stage that we can move to verbal communication and then continue to try and manage the situation non-violently. Open up channels of communication, thank them and use praise appropriately and sensitively if they start to cooperate. Ask them to sit down and see if there can be any compromise or alternative solution to their problems. Always include the other person in trying to resolve the issue so that they feel included and empowered. As any violent situation seems to be diffused or resolved, one final note of caution is to avoid escalating behaviour. So often violence and aggression can be re-triggered or re-inflamed by the wrong word at the wrong time. Avoid criticising the person or belittling them, especially in front of others. Try to be aware not to use unhelpful gestures like pointing which can appear authoritarian or controlling.

Self-defence

No guide to dealing with violence and aggression would be complete without referring to self-defence. Surely we all have the right to use legitimate force to protect ourselves from violent attack? The answer is yes, but within the limitations of what is deemed to be both necessary and reasonable. Here a sense of proportionality must come into effect. Thus, in considering what force is necessary, we must take into account what is reasonable. For example, it may be considered both necessary and reasonable to use force which may seriously injure or even kill someone when faced with the real possibility that your own life is endangered, but it could hardly be justifiable when responding to verbal insults or spitting, however unpleasant these may be. In order to help define 'necessary' and 'reasonable', a number of factors should be considered: the gravity of the crime being prevented, whether it was possible to prevent it using non-violent methods, whether you were willing to try those means first, and finally the relative strength of the persons involved.[1] Alternatives considered by some organisations, projects and individuals are implementing training in breakaway techniques or developing the use of control and restraint. This is the Home Office-approved technique for the management of violence in the prison system which has also been adapted to many healthcare settings. While each has their uses, they also have significant limitations. Breakaway techniques can be both complex and varied, and in the heightened atmosphere of a physical attack a victim would easily become confused in their application.[2] Would you be able to remember more than a handful of techniques for very specific situations? Control and restraint is only applicable in certain settings and it would be unwise to try to replicate it in church or voluntary settings. It is taught by approved trainers over a period of anything from up to two days to a week with specific follow-up refresher training. Given the disadvantages of its specific training, its potential misuse and even the possibility of escalating violence if applied inappropriately,[3] it is not really a suitable strategy or response by individual workers, clergy, small projects and churches. So, broadly speaking, while it is both desirable and fair to say we all have the right to self-defence and to use physical force to protect ourselves when we are faced with violent, physical attack, this needs to be tempered with the notions of what is both reasonable and necessary, and the inherent difficulties in deciding what falls within the parameters of these terms.

Witnessing an attack on another person

As has been stated above, a key factor in safety or reducing risk of violent attack is working with another person rather than in isolation. Given this, it is worthwhile to consider how to respond if you witness aggressive behaviour or even a violent attack directed at a colleague. The first principle is always to

1. Dawes, M. and Winn, D. (1999). 'Managing the monkey: How to defuse the conflicts that can lead to violence in the workplace' p. 57. (Hailsham, East Sussex: The Therapist Ltd)
2. Dawes, M. and Winn, D. (1999). 'Managing the monkey: How to defuse the conflicts that can lead to violence in the workplace' p. 62 (Hailsham, East Sussex: The Therapist Ltd)
3. Mason, T. and Chandley, M. (1999). *Managing Violence and Aggression: A manual for nurses and health care workers* (Edinburgh: Churchill Livingstone), p. 157.

raise the alarm. Let others know what is happening and either call for the appropriate backup and support (which obviously may include the police) or ensure someone else is doing this. Only then is it helpful to make any direct intervention to support the person being attacked. This can appear to be callous, but it is better to ensure that help is on its way before, in a worst-case scenario, there are two people trapped by a violent aggressor. Any immediate intervention is best taken from a safe distance. Let the aggressor know that you are present and are witnessing the incident. If direct physical harm is being inflicted, or the victim is being physically restrained, repeatedly tell the aggressor to stop or let the person go. Final consideration can be given to physical interventions such as dragging the aggressor off the victim, disarming them or using restraint. Firstly it is essential that any such action and intervention is thought out carefully to ensure there will not simply be two victims rather than one. In addition, notions of reasonable force and proportionality, as discussed above, would come into play. If you intervene physically and your colleague is freed to help you in restraining the initial aggressor, consideration must be given to the relative strength of the two parties involved – it is now two against one. Again what was the severity of the crime being prevented and did you use non-violent means first? It is worthwhile to remember at all times that your physical presence alone is a significant factor in reducing the possibility of violent attack.

The responses outlined above are deliberately non-aggressive but *not* passive or weak. They do not rely on practical security measures. They are simple and don't require physical training or regular practice such as are necessary in self-defence or with breakaway techniques. However, it is worthwhile to consider training in the management of violence and aggression. Numerous courses can be offered both to individuals or bought in to train groups of staff and can be tailored to specific situations and settings. When considering attending or buying in training, *do* check that the training organisation and individual trainers understand the sensitivities of churches or specific voluntary projects and indeed their limitations. The internet, local voluntary sector advisory or umbrella agencies, local authorities and local training providers and consortiums are useful places to start to find appropriate resources.

What to do after a serious incident

My focus here will be in two parts. Firstly I will briefly consider what support and response needs to be given to a victim of violent attack which is experienced in the course of work or ministry. Secondly I will examine what can be done to treat or respond to people who are highly aggressive and who routinely use threat and violence. In considering the aggressive and violent person, by no means do I wish to reduce the importance of responding to the needs of those who are victims of violence: their needs are always paramount. However, in the course of my ministry and working life I have encountered many individuals who regularly become aggressive and even violent, but who deeply regret their violence and would love to find alternative ways of dealing with their feelings and learn different patterns of behaviour.

The victim

Firstly let us consider who might need support or need to take action after an incident of aggression and violence and what needs to happen post-incident. The following people or groups all need to be taken into account:

- The victim
- The victim's family
- Colleagues
- Other people who attend the church or use the services offered
- The wider organisation or church

The primary focus is, of course, the victim. An immediate concern is that they receive any medical or health intervention needed if they have been physically harmed. Secondly it is essential that the victim is debriefed and has an opportunity to talk through what has happened. It is important to do this in the immediate aftermath of the incident so they can calm themselves, but also that at an appropriate time in the future an opportunity is made available for further reflection and, if necessary, counselling. Considerable progress has been made in what is known as Critical Incident

Stress Management. It appears that while people benefit from the opportunity to talk through what has happened, intensive counselling at this stage can be counter-productive as it invites people to loosen their natural defences at a time when they need to maintain them. If, after about six months, the person is still affected by the event, that is the time to offer more thorough therapeutic support.[1] It is also worthwhile to remember the victim's family who can also be very distressed and upset at the news of the incident. Particular concern and intervention is needed if the incident has taken place in the home where the victim and any other family members live.

After a serious violent incident it is important to inform any other people who may work from the same premises such as other employees, ministers, administrators, housekeepers and volunteers. Often such people can also feel vulnerable, even if they were not directly involved in the incident. This is especially the case if the aggressive person has left the premises, not been detained by the police or other authorities, and there is the potential of further threat if they return. Consideration should also be given to alerting neighbouring priests, ministers and projects if it is likely the aggressor may turn up at their homes or premises. (This is also the case with 'con artists' who are skilled at manipulating people who work in the caring professions.)

Remember that all those who use a given project or the whole church community will be affected by a violent incident. Many will simply be concerned; others may be fearful of being vulnerable if they come to the church or the project premises. Church officials in dioceses or other structures and management boards and managers in the voluntary sector also have a responsibility to ensure that appropriate support and any necessary follow-up response is in place after an incident. There should be clear and commonly understood procedures regarding who needs to be informed and what action each person responsible should take. All too often there are no reporting or responding mechanisms in place in church organisations or smaller voluntary projects, which results in incidents of

1. Rothschild, B (February 2005). 'Applying the brakes', *Counselling and Psychotherapy Journal*, 15, 1. Can be retrieved at http://www.saskworld.com/bodymindspirit/edition21/17_article_rothschild.htm

violence not being recorded appropriately or responded to effectively at a managerial or organisational level.

The aggressor

Secondly, there needs to be a brief discussion on the needs of those who are violent – or use violence – and how they can be helped. The reality is that there is little help or treatment available. This is not considered a worthy cause for help and support. However, I do know of people who have been greatly disturbed and upset by their violent tendencies or their willingness to resort to violence – even extreme violence. These people may be disposed to benefit from help if it were available to them.

As we have seen, there is a wide range of complex and often interacting reasons why people may use violence and aggression, and any treatment response would be highly dependent on any individual's specific needs. Additional to this is the focus of the arena in which the person becomes violent – for example, some use violence in the home, others against children or other vulnerable people, and others when under the influence of alcohol and drugs. Specific treatment and interventions are described in other booklets in this series. The reality is that a number of people have difficulty with expressing their anger or frustrations. Due to lack of experience of the range of options in dealing with anger, they may resort to violence or other negative ways of expression. We need to ensure that those who are willing to engage constructively with their behaviour are not further disadvantaged and isolated.[1] Working on an individual basis, some people will respond well to befriending and support schemes, particularly where a relationship can develop to explore feelings and emotions and possible strategies can be suggested to deal with these feelings. Additionally, empowerment and advocacy schemes may be of assistance to individuals to help develop alternative strategies to ensure their needs can be met.

Group-work initiatives, such as anger management, would offer a specific treatment response. However, such initiatives are virtually inaccessible until after an offence has been committed! Therapeutic

1. Braithwaite, R. (2001). *Managing Aggression* (London/New York: Routledge/CommunityCare), p. 167.

groups are offered within the criminal justice system by prison and probation services but in one sense they are being offered too late. Group therapy can be particularly effective in these cases, as people explore their beliefs, feelings and behaviour, and learn strategies for managing their anger and how to become more empathic towards others. Sadly, there is little financial support for this kind of group in the community.

The final sanction is incarceration in a mental health facility or imprisonment, hopefully alongside therapeutic help and rehabilitation and medical or psychiatric intervention. Again, this is usually only available after a violent attack or a potentially serious offence, and is usually only initiated in the most serious of cases.

One of the great sources of sadness for those working with these groups is the difficulty in accessing such treatments and interventions where they actually exist. Most treatment and intervention is only offered within the criminal justice system or more secure aspects of mental health services. Being aware of the few services that might be willing to help and support, and how to refer people to them, could be a critical factor in offering pastoral care to those who struggle with violence.

A Christian response

When writing this booklet came up in conversation with other people, including those who work in ministry, many responded that it was interesting and worthwhile. However people often commented, usually towards the end of the conversation, that while non-violence was a nice theory, in the end there were always situations when you would have to use violence or at least physical force. I don't want to criticise those people or even necessarily disagree, but a belief that the use of violence is inevitable saddens me and, more importantly, leaves me with a real sense of disquiet. I can't help but think that we have a new idolatry of violence which deceives us into thinking in destructive and ultimately aggressive terms.

Walter Wink identifies what he has termed the 'myth of redemptive violence',[1] which has been present in religious and literary writings from the earliest times, from early Babylonian myths to contemporary cartoons. Citing the Babylonian creation myth and the modern Popeye cartoons, he shows that violence is seen as a creative force that ultimately liberates us. He argues that this myth is so successful and strong that it hardly seems mythic at all, but rather simply the way things actually are. 'Redemptive violence gives way to violence as an end in itself. It is no longer a religion that uses violence in the pursuit of order and salvation, but one in which violence has become an aphrodisiac, sheer titillation, an addictive high, a substitute for relationships. Violence is no longer the means to a higher good, namely order; violence becomes the end.'[2]

As has been seen in preceding pages, there are various ways we can choose to respond, or sometimes simply instinctively react, to aggression and violence. In short, a number of frameworks can be identified to describe how we often react.[3] We can choose to avoid violence, remove

1 Wink, W. (November 2007). *Facing the Myth of Redemptive Violence.* Retrieved from http://www.ekklesia.co.uk/content/cpt/article_060823wink.shtml

2. Wink, W. (November 2007). *Facing the Myth of Redemptive Violence.* Retrieved from http://www.ekklesia.co.uk/content/cpt/article_060823wink.shtml

3. Slattery, L., Butigan, K., Pelicaric, V. and Preston-Pile, K. (2005). *Engage: Exploring Nonviolent Living; a study program for learning, practicing and experimenting with the power of creative nonviolence to transform our lives and our world* (Oakland, California: Pace e Bene Press).

ourselves from its presence and isolate ourselves from risk; we can accept or accommodate it, seeing it as inevitable; or we can respond with counter-violence, as the ends justify the means or to ensure that through force justice will be achieved. A fourth and more authentic way is to resist the violence through active non-violence.

Christianity has been identified with all these ways of responding, from pacifism to the use of morally justified violence. Sometimes the accusation of passivism has also been levied at Christians – that is, that we simply stand by passively, neither resisting nor defending ourselves against violence. In reality there has also been a long tradition of active resistance through a spirituality of non-violence, but all too often this tradition has been silenced or smothered by the myth of redemptive violence.

Martin Luther King commented on how difficult it was to get his message of non-violent action understood, when so many people had not heard of its methods. Moreover non-violent action simply did not make sense to them – they were so used to avoiding violence or accommodating violence, or they believed that the only other response was violent resistance. 'We had to make it clear that non-violent resistance is not a method of cowardice. It does resist. It is not a method of stagnating passivity and deadening complacency. The non-violent resister is just as opposed to the evil he is standing against as the violent resister but he resists without violence.'[1]

We can turn to the person of Jesus as an ideal role model for nonviolent resistance. There are many who would wish to dismiss Jesus as accommodating violence and oppression, advocating that his followers turn the other cheek and not resist evil. Yet you can see posters and T-shirts depicting Jesus in the image of the revolutionary Che Guevara with the phrase 'Meek. Mild. As if.' Two sides of the same coin, both of which are equally false. Jesus rejected both absolute passivism and violence, and rather promoted a new third way of active non-violent resistance. Walter Wink points out the scriptural translation and contextual problems of Matthew 5:38-41.[2] An alternative translation of 'Resist not the evildoer'

1. King, M. L. quoted in Washington, J. M. (ed.) (1992). *I Have a Dream: Writings and speeches that changed the world* (San Francisco: Harper San Francisco), p. 30.
2. Wink, W. (2003). *Jesus and Non-Violence: A third way* (Minneapolis: Augsburg Fortress) pp. 10–12.

can be rendered 'Don't react violently against the one who is evil.' He further contests that the platitudes that follow of turning the other cheek, giving your cloak and going the extra mile can all be seen in the context of the audience of Jesus in first-century Palestine. These are direct, cultural references which inspire and call the people to take control and to stand as equals with those who would subjugate them, rather than recommend being meek and submissive. This third way of Jesus – the way of non-violent resistance – resonates with his teachings and example. He calls his followers to love their enemies and to bring about the Gospel. He encourages them to acknowledge their own faults and violence, and to take up their cross in solidarity with him to challenge and overcome oppression.[1] We can add to this the profound social and communitarian dimension, and the objective of Jesus' teaching to transcend the individual and transform the community – if not the whole world. Indeed, we can see how Jesus would want to direct us, along with Martin Luther King, to a very different destination to that of violence. 'The end of violence or the aftermath of violence is bitterness. The aftermath of non-violence is reconciliation and the creation of a beloved community.'[2]

1. Wink, W. (November 2007). *Facing the Myth of Redemptive Violence*. Retrieved from http://www.ekklesia.co.uk/content/cpt/article_060823wink.shtml
2. King, M. L. (1957). 'The Power of Non-Violence.' Retrieved from http://teachingamericanhistory.org/library/index.asp?document=1131

Do's and don'ts

- Do consider the risks of violence and aggression.
- Do take practical steps and consider your security.
- Do when faced with a violent person, stay calm.
- Do signal non-aggression.
- Do try to communicate verbally and negotiate.
- Don't let your guard down, even when thr situation seems close to being resolved.
- Do when feeling vulnerable, ask for assistance.
- Don't assume it will never happen to you.
- Do access appropriate training.

Conclusion

I started by reflecting that there are no easy answers. How anyone reacts when faced with direct violence and aggression needs to be understood and accepted. Christians in daily life should be wary not to set themselves up as saints! We would all like to have more ideal responses or be convinced that we could resist resorting to violence, but we can also recognise in ourselves, if we are honest, that we are subject to anger, frustration and irritability which can be expressed destructively and even violently.

> There is so much focus on the distinction between non-violence and violence, between non-violent people and violent people. But in reality it's not easy to take sides like that. One can never be sure that one is completely on the side of non-violence or that the other person is completely on the side of violence. Non-violence is a direction, not a separating line. It has no boundaries.[1]

As Christians, we should not be debating whether we are non-violent, passivist, pacifist or willing to use morally justified violence in certain settings. Rather we can all agree that we are heading in the direction of non-violence – rejecting violence as a preferred mechanism to achieve goals and its seductive power as a solution to our problems, in favour of active peacemaking and becoming agents of love and genuine encounter with others.

Recommended reading

- Davies, W. and Frude, N. (2000). *Preventing Face-To-Face Violence: dealing with anger and aggression at work* (Leicester: The APT Trust).
- Slattery, L., Butigan, K., Pelicaric, V. and Preston-Pile, K. (2005). *Engage: Exploring Nonviolent Living; a study program for learning, practicing and experimenting with the power of creative nonviolence to transform our lives and our world* (Oakland, California: Pace e Bene Press).

Website

www.nationalchurchwatch.com

1. Thich Nhat Hanh in Slattery, L., Butigan, K., Pelicaric, V. and Preston-Pile, K. (2005). *Engage: Exploring Nonviolent Living A study program for learning, practicing and experimenting with the power of creative nonviolence to transform our lives and our world* (Oakland, California: Pace e Bene Press).

Caring for Yourself

Alison Moore

Introduction

Being involved in a difficult situation as it unfolds is demanding and challenging. It is possible that you are *at this moment* caught up in the kind of situation described in this booklet, and this section is written with you in mind. Among all that can be said about how to take care of yourself as well as those for whom you may be responsible, there are three particularly important points to remember:

- Self-care is important for good leadership and management;
- Self-care is to do with the whole self;
- Self-care usually needs help from someone else.

If you do not have the energy or motivation to read this section, then **please give it to a colleague or friend**, who can read it with you in mind and point you to any parts that might be helpful to you. This part of the booklet is divided into four sections:

- Self-care and normal reactions.
- Ways of approaching sensible self-care.
- A Christian response to the idea of self-care.
- Practical suggestions.

What does self-care look like?

Current phrases like 'work-life balance' imply that we should be leading well-balanced lives. While striving to live 'balanced' lives, it is important to bear in mind that as Christians we are primarily called to be disciples, made in the image of our complex, vibrant God. This calling involves recognising the significance of both the physical and spiritual aspects of our lives. A healthy spirituality involves living our humanity to the full. This means that we live in and through our physiological and our psychological make-up and therefore, when exposed to the stress of a difficult situation, this is where we feel the consequences. Showing the strain does not mean that God doesn't love us, nor that we have been an inadequate Christian.

What is self-care?

Care of self is to do with the whole self

Care of self applies to our physical, mental, emotional, behavioural and spiritual experiences, which are interrelated. For example:

> If you eat too much sugar (*behavioural*), you will crave more (*physical*), and you will think you need more chocolate (*mental*). So you will eat another bar (*behavioural*) and feel guilty (*mental / emotional / spiritual*).
>
> If in a religious service you have a sense of God's love and purpose for you (*spiritual*), your anxiety decreases (*emotional*) and your knotted stomach relaxes (*physical*).

Sensible self-care recognises the links and makes allowances.

Care of self is to do with long-term ways of living

We are physically designed to alternate between stress and rest, tension and relaxation. People who do only one or the other lose touch with their humanity. If a rubber band is left permanently stretched, it will stop working and be thrown away. It lasts longest if it is stored in relaxed mode until needed. Like rubber bands, most people can stretch to function well under stress, and we are designed to do just that. However, when we habitually override the need to rest, we reach a point where we can no longer relax, mentally, emotionally, spiritually, behaviourally or physically.[1]

Care of self will look different in different people

We can be surprised that other people's ways of self-care are different from our own. Introverts withdraw, extroverts seek company; some people are energised by activity, others by tranquillity; some need strenuous physical exercise to clear the mind, others need sleep. Forgetting this, we often try to follow someone else's good advice, rather than trust our own instinct about what we need; or we suggest in vain what will help another.

Care of self is essential for good leadership and management

Managers, like rubber bands, can become useless if habitually overstretched. This can show in different ways:

> *physically,* in exhaustion, sleeplessness, appetite change, minor or major illness;
>
> *emotionally,* in numbness, extreme or inappropriate reactions, inability to notice or respond to others, or to receive feedback;
>
> *mentally,* in skewed thought patterns and illogical approaches, inability to assess situations or to recognise this;
>
> *behaviourally,* by excessive drinking, caffeine intake, extremes of sexual activity, obsession with detail, longer but less productive hours, anger outbursts, irregular eating patterns;
>
> *spiritually,* by avoiding prayer or only praying for miracles, superficial external religious compliance, excessive sense of responsibility and with it guilt that refuses compassion, emphasising some Christian themes more than others, ignoring failure as a route to new possibilities, acting out of pride disguised as responsibility.

1. See Sarah Horsman's helpful work on stress reactions described in Litchfield, K. (2006). *Tend My Flock* (Canterbury Press). See particularly chapter 4 sections 4.28 – 4.31.

People, especially leaders, who are overstressed, are not good for their organisations or for the people they are responsible for. Standards of good practice demand enough self-awareness for competency. As a wise person, you will look out for debilitating signs of stress in yourself, and **ask someone else to keep alert too**.

Normal responses to a difficult situation

Normal initial responses to shock[2]

The term '*shock*' sums up the collection of initial reactions in a difficult situation. As the *whole self* will be affected, physical sensations, behaviours, thoughts and feelings may all be different from normal and fluctuate.

Shock reactions are normal and there for good reason. With a limited amount of energy available, it is as if parts of us 'freeze' temporarily so that other parts can function well. Some of what is frozen will later thaw when there is opportunity, and strong emotions or physical exhaustion can surprise long after the difficult situation is over.

Many people experience shock positively, with adrenalin leading to clarity, decisiveness and more energy than normal. However, too much adrenalin can paralyse thinking processes. Also, because you think you are functioning well, you are less likely to realise when you are not doing so. If others trust you as a competent person, they are unlikely to question your behaviour now. Unwise decisions and difficult consequences can follow.

In the early days of a difficult situation your *role* as leader will be affected as people have greater expectations of you. They will expect you to function competently as normal; to manage the unfolding situation in a wise way; to anticipate and meet the needs of those you are responsible for. You may not meet these expectations.

Your *relationships* too will be affected. As manager, your performance is the focus of other people's interest, advice and quite possibly criticism. During difficult situations, misunderstandings can flourish, and relationships suffer. You can find yourself becoming a different sort of leader from the sort you thought you were.

2. There are many good descriptions of responses to sudden loss. Any book on bereavement will cover this, e.g. Worden, J. W. (2001). *Grief Counselling and Grief Therapy* (Third edition), (Bruner-Routledge). For more detail about shock responses, see the chapter 'Caring for Yourself' in Geary, B. and Bryan, J. (eds) (2008). *The Christian Handbook of Abuse, Addiction and Difficult Behaviour* (Kevin Mayhew Ltd).

In church contexts, the divide between work and personal relationships can be much less clear than in other work situations. Church members may not see the need for your changed role as you manage this unusual situation.

The difficult situation may take a lot of time, and will certainly drain your energy. Home relationships may be robust enough to accommodate a period when you are preoccupied. However, if there are ongoing demands there too (young baby, flatmate in crisis, bereavement, teenagers ...), you might need to explain your limited responses.

Normal mid- to longer-term responses to shock

Once a situation has been dealt with and life is back to normal, the relief can lead us to believe prematurely that we are quite back to normal ourselves. As our perception may still be out of sorts, we may not notice how much we are still affected.

Also at this stage the delayed emotional and physical reactions from the initial 'shock' phase can kick in, bringing waves of tiredness. Even two or three years after a seriously difficult situation, a loss of confidence can still be felt.

The impact on *role* and *relationships* is going to be just as strong, but possibly less obvious than at the start. Perhaps your situation simply cannot be resolved, so that instead of your usual role as 'fixer', you have to develop a new role of 'container'. Others in the organisation are likely to forget that the leader is still affected by the ongoing effects of the situation (for example, complicated confidentiality issues may remain). Relationships can change as a result.

What does 'normal' mean for me?

My 'normal' is likely to be different from yours, not just because of our different situations, but also because our individual reactions will differ depending on our personality and how we usually function.[3]

3. The Gilmore Fraleigh 'Style Profile' work is easily accessible and makes a useful distinction between typical reactions when life is calm and when it is stormy. See, for example, Gilmore, S. K. and Fraleigh, P. W. (2004). *Style Profile for Communication at Work* (USA: Friendly Press). The Mennonite Centre in London has a good book service. www.metanoiabooks.org.uk

Approaching self-care

As you face this difficult situation, particularly if you are a manager or leader, some of the following are likely to be true:

- you experience a loss of control – of your diary if nothing else
- you are on a steep learning curve – this may be the first time you have dealt with anything like this
- your overall workload increases – your 'day job' still needs you
- you need to be extra alert – as you might be operating at the edge of your competency
- you need to reflect but there is little opportunity for this – but everyone still expects you to act wisely
- you are bound to fail – to make the *right* decisions at the *right* time in the *right* way for everyone.

However pressurised you feel as you face this difficult situation, it makes sense to step back briefly. By assessing, or 'mapping', both the situation and yourself you will make a better job of leadership.

Mapping the situation

Assessing the demands of the difficult situation and the resources available[4]

It helps to be clear where the lines of responsibility lie between the people involved, both inside and outside your organisation. Clarity about role is useful too. You might need to have different roles, possibly incompatible, at different times and in different relationships. Churches in particular are often unclear organisations, with a volunteering culture that can take good practice for granted rather than setting out clear guidelines. Methodically answering the following questions, preferably with someone else's help,

4. For more detailed suggestions of structured ways of mapping the elements of the situation see the chapter 'Caring for Yourself' in Geary, B. and Bryan, J. (eds) (2008). *The Christian Handbook of Abuse, Addiction and Difficult Behaviour* (Kevin Mayhew Ltd).

will clarify your role and responsibility:

- *Who* and *what* are being affected by this situation?
- What are the *needs* of each person or project?
- *Whose responsibility* is it to meet each of these?

You should now be able to see two things clearly:

Which needs are *not* being met.

Where *your* responsibilities lie.

This in turn will remind you who needs to be briefed about what, what you need from senior management and what support you can offer to junior colleagues.

The Drama Triangle

This schematic way of analysing situations can be very helpful when you are trying to map a difficult situation, particularly when things seem stuck, or you find yourself responding in ways you are not happy with. As its name suggests, the 'drama triangle' looks at the role people *actually* find themselves playing rather than the role they *think* they are taking.

Without realising it, people slip into one of the three positions shown in the drama triangle, '**persecutor**', '**rescuer**' or '**victim**'. They then find that they are thinking and feeling just what the named role suggests. The added difficulty is that the roles can quickly swap round. If you can spot which role you are playing, you are well on the way to being able to do something positive about it.

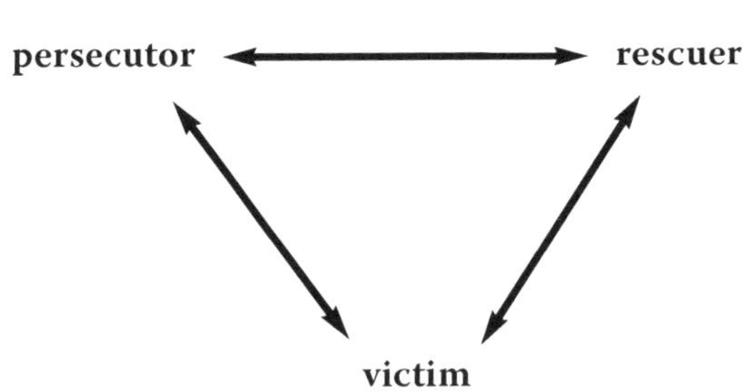

- When you are in '**victim**' role, you act as if you do not have the resources to solve the problem, you feel without thinking;
- when '**rescuer**' you take too much responsibility for someone else and ignore your own needs;
- as '**persecutor**' you are absorbed in your own needs and disregard others.

To change this into a 'winners' triangle' one of the three players must stop trying to change the others and concentrate on changing their own behaviour. The 'winners' triangle' shows how each player can make a change:[5]

- the **victim** can become **vulnerable** i.e. you recognise the strong feelings, but think about how to get help to do something about it;
- the **rescuer** can become **caring** i.e. you show concern and offer help, but within your own limits and without taking over;
- the **persecutor** can become **assertive** i.e. you find ways of meeting your own needs, but without disregarding others.

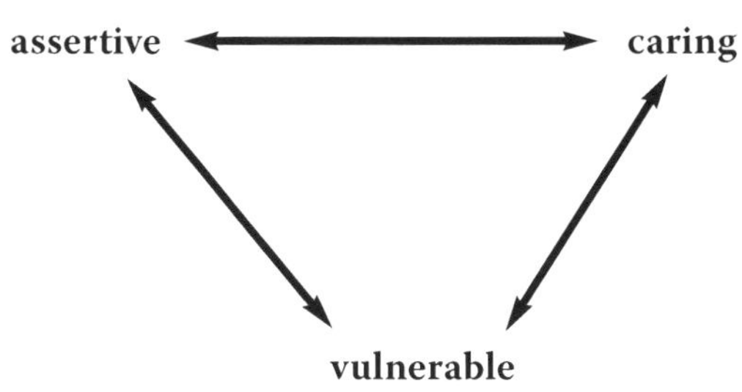

5. For a worked example of the drama/winner triangle see the chapter 'Caring for Yourself' in Geary, B. and Bryan, J. (eds) (2008). *The Christian Handbook of Abuse, Addiction and Difficult Behaviour* (Kevin Mayhew Ltd).

Mapping yourself

Personality

It is useful to know how you function under normal and stressful conditions, and what resources *you* need to work best. You might already be familiar with this through a personality-typing theory.[6] If you are not sure what you are normally like, especially when in a leadership role, or whether you change under stress, just ask a friend or colleague what they have noticed.

This can help you and those around you to make sure that you access the right sort of resources in a difficult situation. What you need might not be obvious to you or those around you. It helps, too, to know what you want from others when you are in stress conditions. For example, do you prefer to delegate or retain control, prefer company or solitude, helpful suggestions or silence? If everyone has realistic expectations then many crossed wires (and cross exchanges) can be avoided.

Relevant past experiences

If you have gone through difficult situations before, you will bring the learning from that into the present. Reflecting on how you responded can help, because even if the current *situation* is completely different, your instinctive *reaction* might be the same. If that reaction worked well, you can trust yourself to act the same way now. But if it did not, you will want to think about how to do things differently this time. For example, if your instinct in a previous difficult situation was to plough through alone and this led to a breakdown of health, you will need this time to act against your instinct and make sure you enlist support.

Even minor past experiences that we are unaware of can impact on the present. When the *dynamic* in a current situation is similar to something we have experienced previously, we can *react* in a similar way. For example, Jill's teenage years were full of conflict with her father whom she saw as domineering and dogmatic. Now a junior minister in a large church, she often argues with her senior male colleague.

6. Most familiar are Myers-Briggs Type Indicator and the Enneagram. Gilmore Fraleigh is more concerned with communication styles than personality.

Relevant current experiences

The dynamic of current experiences can also have an impact, with significant events in your private life affecting how you experience the current difficult situation. This is like a kind of subterranean crossover, experienced emotionally rather than rationally. For example, Val was surprised at the vehement rage she felt towards her team member who had been arrested, accused of financial irregularities. A friend pointed out that it was only six months since Val's husband had left her for someone else, clearing their joint account as he went.

Outside help

The goal of self-care is to manage our lives and work in such a way that seeking outside help when appropriate is simply a normal part of how we live. It is sensible to identify someone you can talk to, for example a friend, line-manager, supervisor or spiritual director, when you need to vent, explore options, or reflect on how you have handled a problem.

Non-managerial supervision

Many people in ministry and other professions with a strong people focus are making use of what counsellors have practised for years – non-managerial supervision, or 'consultative support'. This is a relationship where you can reflect in a structured way on work issues and their impact on you. This benefits both you and your workplace.

Coaching

Coaching is a relatively new area. Working with a coach can help to improve work-life balance, identify goals for development, and explore aspects of yourself that block progress. Although you are unlikely to embark on a coaching relationship while in the midst of a difficult situation, you could use it later to process your experience.

Burnout

Many individuals who work in the caring professions, especially those with responsibility for management, can suffer from burnout. Burnout happens slowly, involving emotional exhaustion with a slow erosion of spirit, loss of idealism and lack of belief that your contribution makes any difference.[7] In common with other stress reactions described earlier, burnout can be obvious to everyone except the person suffering it. For someone already near burnout, having to manage a difficult situation can be the last straw. Treatment for someone in this situation will involve consulting a GP, probably followed by time off work, and individual and/or group therapy.

7. Loudon, S. H. and Francis, L. J. (2003). *The Naked Parish Priest* (London: Continuum).

A Christian response

Christians have mixed reactions to the idea of 'self-care', thinking that the biblical evidence 'take up your cross, lay down your life etc.' mostly argues against it. Many loving Christians encourage others to care for self, while patently not applying this to themselves. Even those who really believe in it can find it difficult to live it in our multi-demanding society.

Of course, we are promised strength beyond what seems humanly possible, and many Christians will testify to this. But this doesn't shortcut the reality that we are physical and psychological human beings. We are still likely to feel deep exhaustion after a challenging set of circumstances, however upheld we were during them. When Elijah fled for his life and wanted to die, God met him in the profound spiritual experience of the 'still small voice' and sent him back to recruit Elisha. But first he had to regain his strength with plenty of sleep and food.[8]

While it is true that self-denial is an important part of Christian discipleship, it is also true that at the heart of Christian faith is the promise of full and joyful living. This is life lived in proper perspective, acknowledging that power, wisdom and love are sourced in God, seen and claimed in Christ and experienced through the Spirit. The joyful Christian disciple takes in as well as giving out, reflects as well as acts. The second commandment is 'Love your neighbour *as yourself*.' This carries a wise psychological insight, that how we treat ourselves is linked with how we are able to treat others.

In other words 'self-care' is *not* the same as 'selfish'.

8. See 1 Kings 19:1-18

Practical suggestions

This section is set out as lists of suggestions so that you can see quickly what might be relevant to you or someone you know. There is some overlap between the lists.

Be realistic

- Life will be different for a while with the inevitable invasiveness of the situation.
- You will be tired and sleep might be broken.
- Eating patterns might change.
- Using stimulants to keep going or alcohol to relax can help *but* ask someone to alert you if you are becoming dependent on them.
- Emotions may well fluctuate more than your normal pattern.
- Prayer may be affected, so ask someone trustworthy to pray on your behalf.
- Normal habits and routines might not work.

Remember

- The big picture – what has God called you to and what do you value most in life?
- If possible do some of what normally helps to keep you sane.
- Stay in touch with people and writings that are good, particularly if there is evil and violence involved.
- Keep your world bigger than the difficult situation[9] – children are useful here.

9. Jerusha Hull McCormack describes this in her book *Grieving – A Beginner's Guide* (Darton, Longman and Todd, 2006). Instead of waiting for the grief – or, in this case, the difficult situation – to diminish in order to have space in life for other things, she suggests deliberately enlarging your world so that the grief or difficult situation does not completely fill it.

- Be creative, even for half an hour, by giving your full attention to music, sport, weeding, DIY ...
- Humour and laughter can vent the most difficult of emotions.
- Routine, not necessarily daily, can help.
- Self-awareness and self-regulation will stand you in good stead.
- Symbolic 'cut-off' points can keep the situation separate from personal life, e.g. a change of clothes or a particular prayer.

Be sensible

- Avoid email communication whenever possible, as the 'send' button cannot be cancelled.
- Delegate, for example by asking someone else to be spokesperson.
- Prioritise, asking for help if you cannot see how to do this.
- Check your opinions and decisions with someone whose judgement you trust.
- Find allies who can help protect you and others from your limitations.

Find support

- Identifying personal support is a sign of strength, not weakness.
- If support from senior personnel is lacking, consider requesting it or explore other options.
- Colleagues and staff might need suggestions for how best to support you.
- Family and friends' ideas of support may be different from yours, so check.

If the difficult situation is in the public arena

- Check that you are using all the resources that are available to you.
- Be on your guard when with other professionals, as the needs of those caught up in the situation can get disregarded in the agendas of the 'experts.'
- Take advice before responding to the media and give yourself time by saying, 'I'll ring you back in ten minutes.'
- Be resigned to the fact that you can't exit from the public arena.
- Stick to your own particular role.
- Know who is responsible for the victim, the perpetrator, the organisation, the other people in the organisation.
- Expect misunderstanding and criticism.

Do I talk about it?

- Some talk is essential – you need someone to be a sounding board.
- Some talk is optional – offloading on someone outside the situation.
- Communication inside and outside the organisation needs careful thought.
- Give yourself time to think by always using the answerphone.
- Conserve emotional energy by giving brief answers when asked about the situation. 'It's very challenging,' 'I am fairly exhausted,' 'We're doing what we can.' Don't go into detail.
- Check with your partner if and how you will talk about it at home. Talk late at night or in your bedroom can be particularly invasive.

If the difficult situation is in a church context

- Although you are the minister, remember that you are not God.
- Although you know you are not God, remember that others will expect you to be.

Listen to your whole self

- Whatever your inner emotions and thoughts, maintain a 'non-anxious presence'[10] for others by breathing deeply, and deliberately relaxing muscles that are tense.
- Notice what you are thinking and what you are feeling.
- Aches in your body will give you clues about the stress you are carrying. Recognising their existence will help.
- Acknowledge the discomfort of conflicting emotions and thoughts.
- Be kind to yourself rather than blaming yourself.
- Stay connected – with yourself and with others.
- Be prepared for the long haul – this is likely to take longer than you anticipate.
- Emotional energy drains physical energy.
- Look for a way of processing the experience later when there's opportunity.

Conclusion

Far from being self-indulgent, self-care is both necessary and godly and a certain amount of self-awareness is helpful. Even under pressure it is worth taking a step back, with the help of someone else, to assess both the situation and yourself. Dealing with a difficult situation will probably take

10. This phrase is used to describe what a mediator offers in conflict transformation work. It provides a succinct summary of what a good leader can offer during a difficult situation.

more out of you than you would think possible – emotionally, physically, mentally and spiritually. Make allowances for a recovery period when the repercussions will go on making an impact.

When you hold a managerial or leadership role you owe it to your staff, colleagues or congregations as well as to yourself, your family and friends, to look after yourself enough to be competent and safe. If this applies to the daily challenge of finding a Christian path in our multi-demanding organisations, it surely applies even more when we face an out-of-the-ordinary difficult situation.

Further reading

- Dr Ruth Fowke has written very accessible short books that look at the issues of stress and Christian faith e.g. *The Last Straw* (Eagle, 2000).
- Daniel Goleman's *Emotional Intelligence* (Bloomsbury, 1996) is the classic on the importance of taking whole-person responses seriously.
- Robert J. Wicks has written a book for counsellors and mental health professionals entitled *The Resilient Counsellor* (Oxford University Press, 2008). It contains wise advice for all managers and clergy who find themselves in stressful situations.
- For those working in churches and other Christian organisations, the Alban Institute, an American publisher, has an excellent range of books on 'practical knowledge in leadership and congregational life'. www.alban.org/bookstore